THIS BOOK BELONGS TO:

_____
_____

EMERGENCY CONACT

_____
_____

Copyright © Teresa Rother

All rights reserved. No part of this publication may be reproduced, distributed, or transmitted in any form or by any means, including photocopy, recording, or other electronic or mechanical methods.

DEDICATION

My First Hiking Journal is dedicated to all children who want to track their hiking and backpacking experiences in a fun and organized way. Recording your hikes will help you enjoy your adventure and allow you to keep a record of each trail.

You are my inspiration for producing this book and I'm honored to be a part of your record-keeping and hiking experience.

HOW TO USE THIS BOOK

This My First Hiking Journal will help guide you by accurately recording each hike and documenting your experience as well as jotting down your favorite memories.

Here are examples of tracking and prompts for you to fill in and write the details of your experience: hiking trail, location, start time, and much more.

Fill in the following information:

1. Date
2. Trail/Location
3. Start time, End time, Duration
4. Terrain
5. Companion list
6. Trail condition and weather
7. Trail notes
8. 5 things I discovered on the trail
9. Top 5 things I like about the trail
10. Sketch space
11. Photo space
12. Difficulty rating
13. Overall rating

DATE _____ START TIME _____ END TIME _____
HIKE/TRAIL NAME _____ DURATION _____
LOCATION _____
TERRAIN _____
COMPANIONS _____

TRAIL CONDITIONS

_____
_____

WEATHER

TRAIL NOTES

_____
_____
_____
_____

5 THINGS I DISCOVERED ON THE TRAIL	TOP 5 THINGS I LIKE ABOUT THE TRAIL

SKETCH	PHOTO

DIFFICULTY

DATE _____ START TIME _____ END TIME _____
HIKE/TRAIL NAME _____ DURATION _____
LOCATION _____
TERRAIN _____
COMPANIONS _____

TRAIL CONDITIONS   WEATHER

TRAIL NOTES

---

5 THINGS I DISCOVERED ON THE TRAIL | TOP 5 THINGS I LIKE ABOUT THE TRAIL

SKETCH | PHOTO

DIFFICULTY  OVERALL RATING

DATE _____
HIKE/TRAIL NAME _____
LOCATION _____
TERRAIN _____
COMPANIONS _____

START TIME _____ END TIME _____
DURATION _____

TRAIL CONDITIONS
_____
_____
_____

WEATHER

TRAIL NOTES
_____
_____
_____
_____
_____

5 THINGS I DISCOVERED ON THE TRAIL
_____
_____
_____
_____
_____

TOP 5 THINGS I LIKE ABOUT THE TRAIL
_____
_____
_____
_____
_____

SKETCH

PHOTO

DIFFICULTY    OVERALL RATING

DATE _____ START TIME _____ END TIME _____
HIKE/TRAIL NAME _____ DURATION _____
LOCATION _____
TERRAIN _____
COMPANIONS _____

TRAIL CONDITIONS

_____
_____
_____

WEATHER

TRAIL NOTES

_____
_____
_____
_____

5 THINGS I DISCOVERED ON THE TRAIL	TOP 5 THINGS I LIKE ABOUT THE TRAIL

SKETCH	PHOTO

DIFFICULTY    OVERALL RATING

DATE _____ START TIME _____ END TIME _____
HIKE/TRAIL NAME _____ DURATION _____
LOCATION _____
TERRAIN _____
COMPANIONS _____

TRAIL CONDITIONS
_____
_____
_____

WEATHER

TRAIL NOTES
_____
_____
_____
_____
_____

5 THINGS I DISCOVERED ON THE TRAIL	TOP 5 THINGS I LIKE ABOUT THE TRAIL
_____	_____
_____	_____
_____	_____
_____	_____
_____	_____

SKETCH	PHOTO

DIFFICULTY   OVERALL RATING

DATE _____
HIKE/TRAIL NAME _____
LOCATION _____
TERRAIN _____
COMPANIONS _____

START TIME _____ END TIME _____
DURATION _____

TRAIL CONDITIONS

WEATHER

TRAIL NOTES

5 THINGS I DISCOVERED ON THE TRAIL

TOP 5 THINGS I LIKE ABOUT THE TRAIL

SKETCH

PHOTO

DIFFICULTY ☆ ☆ ☆ ☆ ☆ OVERALL RATING ☆ ☆ ☆ ☆ ☆

DATE _____ START TIME _____ END TIME _____
HIKE/TRAIL NAME _____ DURATION _____
LOCATION _____
TERRAIN _____
COMPANIONS _____

TRAIL CONDITIONS

_____
_____

WEATHER

TRAIL NOTES

_____
_____
_____
_____

5 THINGS I DISCOVERED ON THE TRAIL	TOP 5 THINGS I LIKE ABOUT THE TRAIL

SKETCH	PHOTO

DIFFICULTY ☆ ☆ ☆ ☆ ☆ OVERALL RATING ☆ ☆ ☆ ☆ ☆

DATE _____ START TIME _____ END TIME _____
HIKE/TRAIL NAME _____ DURATION _____
LOCATION _____
TERRAIN _____
COMPANIONS _____

TRAIL CONDITIONS   WEATHER
_____
_____
_____

TRAIL NOTES
_____
_____
_____
_____

5 THINGS I DISCOVERED ON THE TRAIL | TOP 5 THINGS I LIKE ABOUT THE TRAIL

SKETCH | PHOTO

DIFFICULTY    OVERALL RATING

DATE _____ START TIME _____ END TIME _____
HIKE/TRAIL NAME _____ DURATION _____
LOCATION _____
TERRAIN _____
COMPANIONS _____

TRAIL CONDITIONS
_____
_____
_____

WEATHER

TRAIL NOTES
_____
_____
_____
_____
_____

5 THINGS I DISCOVERED ON THE TRAIL
_____
_____
_____
_____
_____

TOP 5 THINGS I LIKE ABOUT THE TRAIL
_____
_____
_____
_____
_____

SKETCH

PHOTO

DIFFICULTY   OVERALL RATING

DATE _____ START TIME _____ END TIME _____
HIKE/TRAIL NAME _____ DURATION _____
LOCATION _____
TERRAIN _____
COMPANIONS _____

TRAIL CONDITIONS

_____
_____
_____

WEATHER

TRAIL NOTES

_____
_____
_____
_____
_____

5 THINGS I DISCOVERED ON THE TRAIL	TOP 5 THINGS I LIKE ABOUT THE TRAIL

SKETCH

PHOTO

DIFFICULTY ☆ ☆ ☆ ☆ ☆ OVERALL RATING ☆ ☆ ☆ ☆ ☆

DATE _____ START TIME _____ END TIME _____
HIKE/TRAIL NAME _____ DURATION _____
LOCATION _____
TERRAIN _____
COMPANIONS _____

TRAIL CONDITIONS
_____
_____
_____

WEATHER

TRAIL NOTES
_____
_____
_____
_____
_____

5 THINGS I DISCOVERED ON THE TRAIL
_____
_____
_____
_____
_____

TOP 5 THINGS I LIKE ABOUT THE TRAIL
_____
_____
_____
_____
_____

SKETCH

PHOTO

DIFFICULTY  OVERALL RATING

DATE _____ START TIME _____ END TIME _____
HIKE/TRAIL NAME _____ DURATION _____
LOCATION _____
TERRAIN _____
COMPANIONS _____

TRAIL CONDITIONS
_____
_____
_____

WEATHER

TRAIL NOTES
_____
_____
_____
_____

5 THINGS I DISCOVERED ON THE TRAIL
_____
_____
_____
_____
_____

TOP 5 THINGS I LIKE ABOUT THE TRAIL
_____
_____
_____
_____
_____

SKETCH

PHOTO

DIFFICULTY ☆ ☆ ☆ ☆ ☆ OVERALL RATING ☆ ☆ ☆ ☆ ☆

DATE _____ START TIME _____ END TIME _____
HIKE/TRAIL NAME _____ DURATION _____
LOCATION _____
TERRAIN _____
COMPANIONS _____

TRAIL CONDITIONS
_____
_____

WEATHER

TRAIL NOTES
_____
_____
_____
_____

5 THINGS I DISCOVERED ON THE TRAIL	TOP 5 THINGS I LIKE ABOUT THE TRAIL

SKETCH	PHOTO

DIFFICULTY ☆ ☆ ☆ ☆ ☆ OVERALL RATING ☆ ☆ ☆ ☆ ☆

DATE _____ START TIME _____ END TIME _____
HIKE/TRAIL NAME _____ DURATION _____
LOCATION _____
TERRAIN _____
COMPANIONS _____

TRAIL CONDITIONS
_____
_____
_____

WEATHER

TRAIL NOTES
_____
_____
_____
_____
_____

5 THINGS I DISCOVERED ON THE TRAIL	TOP 5 THINGS I LIKE ABOUT THE TRAIL

SKETCH	PHOTO

DIFFICULTY ☆ ☆ ☆ ☆ ☆ OVERALL RATING ☆ ☆ ☆ ☆ ☆

DATE _____ START TIME _____ END TIME _____
HIKE/TRAIL NAME _____ DURATION _____
LOCATION _____
TERRAIN _____
COMPANIONS _____

TRAIL CONDITIONS
_____
_____
_____

WEATHER

TRAIL NOTES
_____
_____
_____
_____
_____

5 THINGS I DISCOVERED ON THE TRAIL	TOP 5 THINGS I LIKE ABOUT THE TRAIL

SKETCH	PHOTO

DIFFICULTY ☆ ☆ ☆ ☆ ☆ OVERALL RATING ☆ ☆ ☆ ☆ ☆

DATE _____   START TIME _____ END TIME _____
HIKE/TRAIL NAME _____ DURATION _____
LOCATION _____
TERRAIN _____
COMPANIONS _____

TRAIL CONDITIONS

_____
_____
_____

WEATHER

TRAIL NOTES

_____
_____
_____
_____
_____

5 THINGS I DISCOVERED ON THE TRAIL	TOP 5 THINGS I LIKE ABOUT THE TRAIL

SKETCH	PHOTO

DIFFICULTY ☆ ☆ ☆ ☆ ☆   OVERALL RATING ☆ ☆ ☆ ☆ ☆

DATE _____ START TIME _____ END TIME _____
HIKE/TRAIL NAME _____ DURATION _____
LOCATION _____
TERRAIN _____
COMPANIONS _____

TRAIL CONDITIONS
_____
_____
_____

WEATHER

TRAIL NOTES
_____
_____
_____
_____
_____

5 THINGS I DISCOVERED ON THE TRAIL
_____
_____
_____
_____
_____

TOP 5 THINGS I LIKE ABOUT THE TRAIL
_____
_____
_____
_____
_____

SKETCH

PHOTO

DIFFICULTY ☆ ☆ ☆ ☆ ☆ OVERALL RATING ☆ ☆ ☆ ☆ ☆

DATE _____ START TIME _____ END TIME _____
HIKE/TRAIL NAME _____ DURATION _____
LOCATION _____
TERRAIN _____
COMPANIONS _____

TRAIL CONDITIONS
_____
_____
_____

WEATHER

TRAIL NOTES
_____
_____
_____
_____
_____

5 THINGS I DISCOVERED ON THE TRAIL	TOP 5 THINGS I LIKE ABOUT THE TRAIL
_____	_____
_____	_____
_____	_____
_____	_____
_____	_____

SKETCH	PHOTO

DIFFICULTY ☆ ☆ ☆ ☆ ☆ OVERALL RATING ☆ ☆ ☆ ☆ ☆

DATE _____ START TIME _____ END TIME _____
HIKE/TRAIL NAME _____ DURATION _____
LOCATION _____
TERRAIN _____
COMPANIONS _____

TRAIL CONDITIONS
_____
_____

WEATHER

TRAIL NOTES
_____
_____
_____
_____

5 THINGS I DISCOVERED ON THE TRAIL	TOP 5 THINGS I LIKE ABOUT THE TRAIL

SKETCH	PHOTO

DIFFICULTY ☆ ☆ ☆ ☆ ☆ OVERALL RATING ☆ ☆ ☆ ☆ ☆

DATE _____ START TIME _____ END TIME _____
HIKE/TRAIL NAME _____ DURATION _____
LOCATION _____
TERRAIN _____
COMPANIONS _____

TRAIL CONDITIONS   WEATHER

TRAIL NOTES

5 THINGS I DISCOVERED ON THE TRAIL | TOP 5 THINGS I LIKE ABOUT THE TRAIL

SKETCH   PHOTO

DIFFICULTY ☆ ☆ ☆ ☆ ☆ OVERALL RATING ☆ ☆ ☆ ☆ ☆

DATE _____ START TIME _____ END TIME _____
HIKE/TRAIL NAME _____ DURATION _____
LOCATION _____
TERRAIN _____
COMPANIONS _____

TRAIL CONDITIONS

WEATHER

TRAIL NOTES

5 THINGS I DISCOVERED ON THE TRAIL

TOP 5 THINGS I LIKE ABOUT THE TRAIL

SKETCH

PHOTO

DIFFICULTY ☆ ☆ ☆ ☆ ☆ OVERALL RATING ☆ ☆ ☆ ☆ ☆

DATE _____ START TIME _____ END TIME _____
HIKE/TRAIL NAME _____ DURATION _____
LOCATION _____
TERRAIN _____
COMPANIONS _____

TRAIL CONDITIONS
_____
_____
_____

WEATHER

TRAIL NOTES
_____
_____
_____
_____

5 THINGS I DISCOVERED ON THE TRAIL	TOP 5 THINGS I LIKE ABOUT THE TRAIL

SKETCH	PHOTO

DIFFICULTY ☆ ☆ ☆ ☆ ☆ OVERALL RATING ☆ ☆ ☆ ☆ ☆

DATE _____ START TIME _____ END TIME _____
HIKE/TRAIL NAME _____ DURATION _____
LOCATION _____
TERRAIN _____
COMPANIONS _____

TRAIL CONDITIONS

_____
_____
_____

WEATHER

TRAIL NOTES

_____
_____
_____
_____
_____

5 THINGS I DISCOVERED ON THE TRAIL	TOP 5 THINGS I LIKE ABOUT THE TRAIL

SKETCH	PHOTO

DIFFICULTY    OVERALL RATING

DATE _____ START TIME _____ END TIME _____
HIKE/TRAIL NAME _____ DURATION _____
LOCATION _____
TERRAIN _____
COMPANIONS _____

TRAIL CONDITIONS
_____
_____
_____

WEATHER

TRAIL NOTES
_____
_____
_____
_____

5 THINGS I DISCOVERED ON THE TRAIL	TOP 5 THINGS I LIKE ABOUT THE TRAIL

SKETCH	PHOTO

DIFFICULTY ☆ ☆ ☆ ☆ ☆ OVERALL RATING ☆ ☆ ☆ ☆ ☆

DATE _____
HIKE/TRAIL NAME _____
LOCATION _____
TERRAIN _____
COMPANIONS _____

START TIME _____ END TIME _____
DURATION _____

TRAIL CONDITIONS

WEATHER

TRAIL NOTES

5 THINGS I DISCOVERED ON THE TRAIL

TOP 5 THINGS I LIKE ABOUT THE TRAIL

SKETCH

PHOTO

DIFFICULTY ☆ ☆ ☆ ☆ ☆ OVERALL RATING ☆ ☆ ☆ ☆ ☆

DATE _____   START TIME _____ END TIME _____
HIKE/TRAIL NAME _____ DURATION _____
LOCATION _____
TERRAIN _____
COMPANIONS _____

TRAIL CONDITIONS

WEATHER

TRAIL NOTES

5 THINGS I DISCOVERED ON THE TRAIL

TOP 5 THINGS I LIKE ABOUT THE TRAIL

SKETCH

PHOTO

DIFFICULTY ☆ ☆ ☆ ☆ ☆ OVERALL RATING ☆ ☆ ☆ ☆ ☆

DATE _____
HIKE/TRAIL NAME _____
LOCATION _____
TERRAIN _____
COMPANIONS _____

START TIME _____ END TIME _____
DURATION _____

TRAIL CONDITIONS

WEATHER

TRAIL NOTES

5 THINGS I DISCOVERED ON THE TRAIL

TOP 5 THINGS I LIKE ABOUT THE TRAIL

SKETCH

PHOTO

DIFFICULTY ☆ ☆ ☆ ☆ ☆ OVERALL RATING ☆ ☆ ☆ ☆ ☆

DATE _____ START TIME _____ END TIME _____
HIKE/TRAIL NAME _____ DURATION _____
LOCATION _____
TERRAIN _____
COMPANIONS _____

TRAIL CONDITIONS   WEATHER

TRAIL NOTES

5 THINGS I DISCOVERED ON THE TRAIL | TOP 5 THINGS I LIKE ABOUT THE TRAIL

SKETCH | PHOTO

DIFFICULTY ☆ ☆ ☆ ☆ ☆ OVERALL RATING ☆ ☆ ☆ ☆ ☆

DATE _____	START TIME _____ END TIME _____
HIKE/TRAIL NAME _____	DURATION _____
LOCATION _____	
TERRAIN _____	
COMPANIONS _____	

TRAIL CONDITIONS

_____
_____
_____

WEATHER

TRAIL NOTES

_____
_____
_____
_____
_____

5 THINGS I DISCOVERED ON THE TRAIL	TOP 5 THINGS I LIKE ABOUT THE TRAIL
_____	_____
_____	_____
_____	_____
_____	_____
_____	_____

SKETCH	PHOTO

DIFFICULTY ☆ ☆ ☆ ☆ ☆ OVERALL RATING ☆ ☆ ☆ ☆ ☆

DATE _____ START TIME _____ END TIME _____
HIKE/TRAIL NAME _____ DURATION _____
LOCATION _____
TERRAIN _____
COMPANIONS _____

TRAIL CONDITIONS   WEATHER

TRAIL NOTES

5 THINGS I DISCOVERED ON THE TRAIL | TOP 5 THINGS I LIKE ABOUT THE TRAIL

SKETCH | PHOTO

DIFFICULTY ☆ ☆ ☆ ☆ ☆ OVERALL RATING ☆ ☆ ☆ ☆ ☆

DATE _____ START TIME _____ END TIME _____
HIKE/TRAIL NAME _____ DURATION _____
LOCATION _____
TERRAIN _____
COMPANIONS _____

TRAIL CONDITIONS
_____
_____

WEATHER

TRAIL NOTES
_____
_____
_____
_____
_____

5 THINGS I DISCOVERED ON THE TRAIL	TOP 5 THINGS I LIKE ABOUT THE TRAIL

SKETCH

PHOTO

DIFFICULTY    OVERALL RATING

DATE _____ START TIME _____ END TIME _____
HIKE/TRAIL NAME _____ DURATION _____
LOCATION _____
TERRAIN _____
COMPANIONS _____

TRAIL CONDITIONS
_____
_____
_____

WEATHER

TRAIL NOTES
_____
_____
_____
_____
_____

5 THINGS I DISCOVERED ON THE TRAIL	TOP 5 THINGS I LIKE ABOUT THE TRAIL

SKETCH	PHOTO

DIFFICULTY ☆ ☆ ☆ ☆ ☆   OVERALL RATING ☆ ☆ ☆ ☆ ☆

DATE _____ START TIME _____ END TIME _____
HIKE/TRAIL NAME _____ DURATION _____
LOCATION _____
TERRAIN _____
COMPANIONS _____

TRAIL CONDITIONS
_____
_____
_____

WEATHER

TRAIL NOTES
_____
_____
_____
_____
_____

5 THINGS I DISCOVERED ON THE TRAIL
_____
_____
_____
_____
_____

TOP 5 THINGS I LIKE ABOUT THE TRAIL
_____
_____
_____
_____
_____

SKETCH

PHOTO

DIFFICULTY ☆ ☆ ☆ ☆ ☆ OVERALL RATING ☆ ☆ ☆ ☆ ☆

DATE _____ START TIME _____ END TIME _____
HIKE/TRAIL NAME _____ DURATION _____
LOCATION _____
TERRAIN _____
COMPANIONS _____

TRAIL CONDITIONS
_____
_____
_____

WEATHER

TRAIL NOTES
_____
_____
_____
_____

5 THINGS I DISCOVERED ON THE TRAIL	TOP 5 THINGS I LIKE ABOUT THE TRAIL

SKETCH	PHOTO

DIFFICULTY ☆ ☆ ☆ ☆ ☆ OVERALL RATING ☆ ☆ ☆ ☆ ☆

DATE _____ START TIME _____ END TIME _____
HIKE/TRAIL NAME _____ DURATION _____
LOCATION _____
TERRAIN _____
COMPANIONS _____

TRAIL CONDITIONS

WEATHER

TRAIL NOTES

5 THINGS I DISCOVERED ON THE TRAIL

TOP 5 THINGS I LIKE ABOUT THE TRAIL

SKETCH

PHOTO

DIFFICULTY ☆ ☆ ☆ ☆ ☆ OVERALL RATING ☆ ☆ ☆ ☆ ☆

DATE _____ START TIME _____ END TIME _____
HIKE/TRAIL NAME _____ DURATION _____
LOCATION _____
TERRAIN _____
COMPANIONS _____

TRAIL CONDITIONS
_____
_____
_____

WEATHER

TRAIL NOTES
_____
_____
_____
_____
_____

5 THINGS I DISCOVERED ON THE TRAIL	TOP 5 THINGS I LIKE ABOUT THE TRAIL
_____	_____
_____	_____
_____	_____
_____	_____
_____	_____

SKETCH	PHOTO

DIFFICULTY ☆ ☆ ☆ ☆ ☆ OVERALL RATING ☆ ☆ ☆ ☆ ☆

DATE _____ START TIME _____ END TIME _____
HIKE/TRAIL NAME _____ DURATION _____
LOCATION _____
TERRAIN _____
COMPANIONS _____

TRAIL CONDITIONS

_____
_____
_____

WEATHER

TRAIL NOTES

_____
_____
_____
_____
_____

5 THINGS I DISCOVERED ON THE TRAIL

_____
_____
_____
_____
_____

TOP 5 THINGS I LIKE ABOUT THE TRAIL

_____
_____
_____
_____
_____

SKETCH

PHOTO

DIFFICULTY ☆ ☆ ☆ ☆ ☆ OVERALL RATING ☆ ☆ ☆ ☆ ☆

DATE _____ START TIME _____ END TIME _____
HIKE/TRAIL NAME _____ DURATION _____
LOCATION _____
TERRAIN _____
COMPANIONS _____

TRAIL CONDITIONS
_____
_____
_____

WEATHER

TRAIL NOTES
_____
_____
_____
_____
_____

5 THINGS I DISCOVERED ON THE TRAIL	TOP 5 THINGS I LIKE ABOUT THE TRAIL

SKETCH

PHOTO

DIFFICULTY ☆ ☆ ☆ ☆ ☆ OVERALL RATING ☆ ☆ ☆ ☆ ☆

DATE _____ START TIME _____ END TIME _____
HIKE/TRAIL NAME _____ DURATION _____
LOCATION _____
TERRAIN _____
COMPANIONS _____

TRAIL CONDITIONS

_____
_____
_____

WEATHER

TRAIL NOTES

_____
_____
_____
_____
_____

5 THINGS I DISCOVERED ON THE TRAIL

_____
_____
_____
_____
_____

TOP 5 THINGS I LIKE ABOUT THE TRAIL

_____
_____
_____
_____
_____

SKETCH

PHOTO

DIFFICULTY ☆ ☆ ☆ ☆ ☆ OVERALL RATING ☆ ☆ ☆ ☆ ☆

DATE _____ START TIME _____ END TIME _____
HIKE/TRAIL NAME _____ DURATION _____
LOCATION _____
TERRAIN _____
COMPANIONS _____

TRAIL CONDITIONS
_____
_____
_____

WEATHER

TRAIL NOTES
_____
_____
_____
_____
_____

5 THINGS I DISCOVERED ON THE TRAIL	TOP 5 THINGS I LIKE ABOUT THE TRAIL

SKETCH	PHOTO

DIFFICULTY ☆ ☆ ☆ ☆ ☆ OVERALL RATING ☆ ☆ ☆ ☆ ☆

DATE _____ START TIME _____ END TIME _____
HIKE/TRAIL NAME _____ DURATION _____
LOCATION _____
TERRAIN _____
COMPANIONS _____

TRAIL CONDITIONS

WEATHER

TRAIL NOTES

5 THINGS I DISCOVERED ON THE TRAIL

TOP 5 THINGS I LIKE ABOUT THE TRAIL

SKETCH

PHOTO

DIFFICULTY ☆ ☆ ☆ ☆ ☆ OVERALL RATING ☆ ☆ ☆ ☆ ☆

DATE _____ START TIME _____ END TIME _____
HIKE/TRAIL NAME _____ DURATION _____
LOCATION _____
TERRAIN _____
COMPANIONS _____

TRAIL CONDITIONS   WEATHER
_____
_____
_____

TRAIL NOTES
_____
_____
_____
_____

5 THINGS I DISCOVERED ON THE TRAIL	TOP 5 THINGS I LIKE ABOUT THE TRAIL

SKETCH	PHOTO

DIFFICULTY ☆ ☆ ☆ ☆ ☆ OVERALL RATING ☆ ☆ ☆ ☆ ☆

DATE _____ START TIME _____ END TIME _____
HIKE/TRAIL NAME _____ DURATION _____
LOCATION _____
TERRAIN _____
COMPANIONS _____

TRAIL CONDITIONS

WEATHER

TRAIL NOTES

5 THINGS I DISCOVERED ON THE TRAIL

TOP 5 THINGS I LIKE ABOUT THE TRAIL

SKETCH

PHOTO

DIFFICULTY ☆ ☆ ☆ ☆ ☆ OVERALL RATING ☆ ☆ ☆ ☆ ☆

DATE _____ START TIME _____ END TIME _____
HIKE/TRAIL NAME _____ DURATION _____
LOCATION _____
TERRAIN _____
COMPANIONS _____

TRAIL CONDITIONS   WEATHER

_____
_____
_____

TRAIL NOTES
_____
_____
_____
_____
_____

5 THINGS I DISCOVERED ON THE TRAIL	TOP 5 THINGS I LIKE ABOUT THE TRAIL

SKETCH	PHOTO

DIFFICULTY ✮ ✮ ✮ ✮ ✮ OVERALL RATING ✮ ✮ ✮ ✮ ✮

DATE _____ START TIME _____ END TIME _____
HIKE/TRAIL NAME _____ DURATION _____
LOCATION _____
TERRAIN _____
COMPANIONS _____

TRAIL CONDITIONS

_____
_____
_____

WEATHER

TRAIL NOTES

_____
_____
_____
_____
_____

5 THINGS I DISCOVERED ON THE TRAIL
_____
_____
_____
_____
_____

TOP 5 THINGS I LIKE ABOUT THE TRAIL
_____
_____
_____
_____
_____

SKETCH

PHOTO

DIFFICULTY ☆ ☆ ☆ ☆ ☆ OVERALL RATING ☆ ☆ ☆ ☆ ☆

DATE _____ START TIME _____ END TIME _____
HIKE/TRAIL NAME _____ DURATION _____
LOCATION _____
TERRAIN _____
COMPANIONS _____

TRAIL CONDITIONS
_____
_____
_____

WEATHER

TRAIL NOTES
_____
_____
_____
_____
_____

5 THINGS I DISCOVERED ON THE TRAIL	TOP 5 THINGS I LIKE ABOUT THE TRAIL

SKETCH	PHOTO

DIFFICULTY ☆ ☆ ☆ ☆ ☆ OVERALL RATING ☆ ☆ ☆ ☆ ☆

DATE _____   START TIME _____ END TIME _____
HIKE/TRAIL NAME _____   DURATION _____
LOCATION _____
TERRAIN _____
COMPANIONS _____

TRAIL CONDITIONS

_____
_____
_____

WEATHER

TRAIL NOTES

_____
_____
_____
_____
_____

5 THINGS I DISCOVERED ON THE TRAIL
_____
_____
_____
_____
_____

TOP 5 THINGS I LIKE ABOUT THE TRAIL
_____
_____
_____
_____
_____

SKETCH

PHOTO

DIFFICULTY ☆ ☆ ☆ ☆ ☆ OVERALL RATING ☆ ☆ ☆ ☆ ☆

DATE _____   START TIME _____ END TIME _____
HIKE/TRAIL NAME _____   DURATION _____
LOCATION _____
TERRAIN _____
COMPANIONS _____

TRAIL CONDITIONS
_____
_____
_____

WEATHER

TRAIL NOTES
_____
_____
_____
_____

5 THINGS I DISCOVERED ON THE TRAIL	TOP 5 THINGS I LIKE ABOUT THE TRAIL
_____	_____
_____	_____
_____	_____
_____	_____
_____	_____

SKETCH	PHOTO

DIFFICULTY ☆ ☆ ☆ ☆ ☆   OVERALL RATING ☆ ☆ ☆ ☆ ☆

DATE _____ START TIME _____ END TIME _____
HIKE/TRAIL NAME _____ DURATION _____
LOCATION _____
TERRAIN _____
COMPANIONS _____

TRAIL CONDITIONS

_____
_____
_____

WEATHER

TRAIL NOTES

_____
_____
_____
_____
_____

5 THINGS I DISCOVERED ON THE TRAIL	TOP 5 THINGS I LIKE ABOUT THE TRAIL

SKETCH

PHOTO

DIFFICULTY ☆ ☆ ☆ ☆ ☆ OVERALL RATING ☆ ☆ ☆ ☆ ☆

DATE _____ START TIME _____ END TIME _____
HIKE/TRAIL NAME _____ DURATION _____
LOCATION _____
TERRAIN _____
COMPANIONS _____

TRAIL CONDITIONS

_____
_____
_____

WEATHER

TRAIL NOTES

_____
_____
_____
_____
_____

5 THINGS I DISCOVERED ON THE TRAIL	TOP 5 THINGS I LIKE ABOUT THE TRAIL

SKETCH	PHOTO

DIFFICULTY ☆ ☆ ☆ ☆ ☆ OVERALL RATING ☆ ☆ ☆ ☆ ☆

DATE _____   START TIME _____ END TIME _____
HIKE/TRAIL NAME _____   DURATION _____
LOCATION _____
TERRAIN _____
COMPANIONS _____

TRAIL CONDITIONS   WEATHER

TRAIL NOTES

5 THINGS I DISCOVERED ON THE TRAIL   TOP 5 THINGS I LIKE ABOUT THE TRAIL

SKETCH   PHOTO

DIFFICULTY ☆ ☆ ☆ ☆ ☆ OVERALL RATING ☆ ☆ ☆ ☆ ☆

DATE _____   START TIME _____ END TIME _____
HIKE/TRAIL NAME _____ DURATION _____
LOCATION _____
TERRAIN _____
COMPANIONS _____

TRAIL CONDITIONS   WEATHER

TRAIL NOTES

5 THINGS I DISCOVERED ON THE TRAIL | TOP 5 THINGS I LIKE ABOUT THE TRAIL

SKETCH   PHOTO

DIFFICULTY ☆ ☆ ☆ ☆ ☆ OVERALL RATING ☆ ☆ ☆ ☆ ☆

DATE _____   START TIME _____ END TIME _____
HIKE/TRAIL NAME _____   DURATION _____
LOCATION _____
TERRAIN _____
COMPANIONS _____

TRAIL CONDITIONS
_____
_____
_____

WEATHER

TRAIL NOTES
_____
_____
_____
_____
_____

5 THINGS I DISCOVERED ON THE TRAIL
_____
_____
_____
_____
_____

TOP 5 THINGS I LIKE ABOUT THE TRAIL
_____
_____
_____
_____
_____

SKETCH

PHOTO

DIFFICULTY    OVERALL RATING

DATE _____ START TIME _____ END TIME _____
HIKE/TRAIL NAME _____ DURATION _____
LOCATION _____
TERRAIN _____
COMPANIONS _____

TRAIL CONDITIONS
_____
_____
_____

WEATHER

TRAIL NOTES
_____
_____
_____
_____
_____

5 THINGS I DISCOVERED ON THE TRAIL	TOP 5 THINGS I LIKE ABOUT THE TRAIL

SKETCH	PHOTO

DIFFICULTY ☆ ☆ ☆ ☆ ☆ OVERALL RATING ☆ ☆ ☆ ☆ ☆

DATE _____ START TIME _____ END TIME _____
HIKE/TRAIL NAME _____ DURATION _____
LOCATION _____
TERRAIN _____
COMPANIONS _____

TRAIL CONDITIONS

_____
_____
_____

WEATHER

TRAIL NOTES

_____
_____
_____
_____
_____

5 THINGS I DISCOVERED ON THE TRAIL

TOP 5 THINGS I LIKE ABOUT THE TRAIL

SKETCH

PHOTO

DIFFICULTY ☆ ☆ ☆ ☆ ☆ OVERALL RATING ☆ ☆ ☆ ☆ ☆

DATE _____ START TIME _____ END TIME _____
HIKE/TRAIL NAME _____ DURATION _____
LOCATION _____
TERRAIN _____
COMPANIONS _____

TRAIL CONDITIONS
_____
_____
_____

WEATHER

TRAIL NOTES
_____
_____
_____
_____

5 THINGS I DISCOVERED ON THE TRAIL
_____
_____
_____
_____
_____

TOP 5 THINGS I LIKE ABOUT THE TRAIL
_____
_____
_____
_____
_____

SKETCH

PHOTO

DIFFICULTY ☆ ☆ ☆ ☆ ☆   OVERALL RATING ☆ ☆ ☆ ☆ ☆

DATE _____ START TIME _____ END TIME _____
HIKE/TRAIL NAME _____ DURATION _____
LOCATION _____
TERRAIN _____
COMPANIONS _____

TRAIL CONDITIONS
_____
_____
_____

WEATHER

TRAIL NOTES
_____
_____
_____
_____
_____

5 THINGS I DISCOVERED ON THE TRAIL	TOP 5 THINGS I LIKE ABOUT THE TRAIL

SKETCH	PHOTO

DIFFICULTY ☆ ☆ ☆ ☆ ☆ OVERALL RATING ☆ ☆ ☆ ☆ ☆

DATE _____ START TIME _____ END TIME _____
HIKE/TRAIL NAME _____ DURATION _____
LOCATION _____
TERRAIN _____
COMPANIONS _____

TRAIL CONDITIONS   WEATHER
_____
_____
_____

TRAIL NOTES
_____
_____
_____
_____
_____

5 THINGS I DISCOVERED ON THE TRAIL	TOP 5 THINGS I LIKE ABOUT THE TRAIL

SKETCH	PHOTO

DIFFICULTY ☆ ☆ ☆ ☆ ☆   OVERALL RATING ☆ ☆ ☆ ☆ ☆

DATE _____ START TIME _____ END TIME _____
HIKE/TRAIL NAME _____ DURATION _____
LOCATION _____
TERRAIN _____
COMPANIONS _____

TRAIL CONDITIONS

_____
_____
_____

WEATHER

TRAIL NOTES

_____
_____
_____
_____
_____

5 THINGS I DISCOVERED ON THE TRAIL	TOP 5 THINGS I LIKE ABOUT THE TRAIL

SKETCH	PHOTO

DIFFICULTY ☆ ☆ ☆ ☆ ☆ OVERALL RATING ☆ ☆ ☆ ☆ ☆

DATE _____ START TIME _____ END TIME _____
HIKE/TRAIL NAME _____ DURATION _____
LOCATION _____
TERRAIN _____
COMPANIONS _____

TRAIL CONDITIONS
_____
_____
_____

WEATHER

TRAIL NOTES
_____
_____
_____
_____

5 THINGS I DISCOVERED ON THE TRAIL	TOP 5 THINGS I LIKE ABOUT THE TRAIL

SKETCH	PHOTO

DIFFICULTY ☆ ☆ ☆ ☆ ☆ OVERALL RATING ☆ ☆ ☆ ☆ ☆

DATE _____
HIKE/TRAIL NAME _____
LOCATION _____
TERRAIN _____
COMPANIONS _____

START TIME _____ END TIME _____
DURATION _____

TRAIL CONDITIONS

_____
_____
_____

WEATHER

TRAIL NOTES

_____
_____
_____
_____
_____

5 THINGS I DISCOVERED ON THE TRAIL

TOP 5 THINGS I LIKE ABOUT THE TRAIL

SKETCH

PHOTO

DIFFICULTY ☆ ☆ ☆ ☆ ☆ OVERALL RATING ☆ ☆ ☆ ☆ ☆

DATE _____ START TIME _____ END TIME _____
HIKE/TRAIL NAME _____ DURATION _____
LOCATION _____
TERRAIN _____
COMPANIONS _____

TRAIL CONDITIONS
_____
_____
_____

WEATHER

TRAIL NOTES
_____
_____
_____
_____
_____

5 THINGS I DISCOVERED ON THE TRAIL	TOP 5 THINGS I LIKE ABOUT THE TRAIL

SKETCH	PHOTO

DIFFICULTY ☆ ☆ ☆ ☆ ☆ OVERALL RATING ☆ ☆ ☆ ☆ ☆

DATE _____ START TIME _____ END TIME _____
HIKE/TRAIL NAME _____ DURATION _____
LOCATION _____
TERRAIN _____
COMPANIONS _____

TRAIL CONDITIONS

WEATHER

TRAIL NOTES

5 THINGS I DISCOVERED ON THE TRAIL | TOP 5 THINGS I LIKE ABOUT THE TRAIL

SKETCH | PHOTO

DIFFICULTY ☆ ☆ ☆ ☆ ☆ OVERALL RATING ☆ ☆ ☆ ☆ ☆

DATE _____ START TIME _____ END TIME _____
HIKE/TRAIL NAME _____ DURATION _____
LOCATION _____
TERRAIN _____
COMPANIONS _____

TRAIL CONDITIONS

_____
_____
_____

WEATHER

TRAIL NOTES

_____
_____
_____
_____
_____

5 THINGS I DISCOVERED ON THE TRAIL	TOP 5 THINGS I LIKE ABOUT THE TRAIL

SKETCH	PHOTO

DIFFICULTY ☆ ☆ ☆ ☆ ☆   OVERALL RATING ☆ ☆ ☆ ☆ ☆

DATE _____ START TIME _____ END TIME _____
HIKE/TRAIL NAME _____ DURATION _____
LOCATION _____
TERRAIN _____
COMPANIONS _____

TRAIL CONDITIONS

_____

_____

_____

WEATHER

TRAIL NOTES

_____
_____
_____
_____
_____

5 THINGS I DISCOVERED ON THE TRAIL	TOP 5 THINGS I LIKE ABOUT THE TRAIL

SKETCH	PHOTO

DIFFICULTY  OVERALL RATING

DATE _____ START TIME _____ END TIME _____
HIKE/TRAIL NAME _____ DURATION _____
LOCATION _____
TERRAIN _____
COMPANIONS _____

TRAIL CONDITIONS

WEATHER

TRAIL NOTES

5 THINGS I DISCOVERED ON THE TRAIL

TOP 5 THINGS I LIKE ABOUT THE TRAIL

SKETCH

PHOTO

DIFFICULTY ☆ ☆ ☆ ☆ ☆ OVERALL RATING ☆ ☆ ☆ ☆ ☆

DATE _____   START TIME _____ END TIME _____
HIKE/TRAIL NAME _____   DURATION _____
LOCATION _____
TERRAIN _____
COMPANIONS _____

TRAIL CONDITIONS
_____
_____
_____

WEATHER

TRAIL NOTES
_____
_____
_____
_____
_____

5 THINGS I DISCOVERED ON THE TRAIL	TOP 5 THINGS I LIKE ABOUT THE TRAIL

SKETCH	PHOTO

DIFFICULTY  OVERALL RATING

DATE _____ START TIME _____ END TIME _____
HIKE/TRAIL NAME _____ DURATION _____
LOCATION _____
TERRAIN _____
COMPANIONS _____

TRAIL CONDITIONS
_____
_____
_____

WEATHER

TRAIL NOTES
_____
_____
_____
_____

5 THINGS I DISCOVERED ON THE TRAIL
_____
_____
_____
_____
_____

TOP 5 THINGS I LIKE ABOUT THE TRAIL
_____
_____
_____
_____
_____

SKETCH

PHOTO

DIFFICULTY ☆ ☆ ☆ ☆ ☆ OVERALL RATING ☆ ☆ ☆ ☆ ☆

DATE _____   START TIME _____ END TIME _____
HIKE/TRAIL NAME _____   DURATION _____
LOCATION _____
TERRAIN _____
COMPANIONS _____

TRAIL CONDITIONS
_____
_____
_____

WEATHER

TRAIL NOTES
_____
_____
_____
_____
_____

5 THINGS I DISCOVERED ON THE TRAIL
_____
_____
_____
_____
_____

TOP 5 THINGS I LIKE ABOUT THE TRAIL
_____
_____
_____
_____
_____

SKETCH

PHOTO

DIFFICULTY ☆ ☆ ☆ ☆ ☆   OVERALL RATING ☆ ☆ ☆ ☆ ☆

DATE _____ START TIME _____ END TIME _____
HIKE/TRAIL NAME _____ DURATION _____
LOCATION _____
TERRAIN _____
COMPANIONS _____

TRAIL CONDITIONS
_____
_____
_____

WEATHER

TRAIL NOTES
_____
_____
_____
_____

5 THINGS I DISCOVERED ON THE TRAIL
_____
_____
_____
_____
_____

TOP 5 THINGS I LIKE ABOUT THE TRAIL
_____
_____
_____
_____
_____

SKETCH

PHOTO

DIFFICULTY ☆ ☆ ☆ ☆ ☆ OVERALL RATING ☆ ☆ ☆ ☆ ☆

DATE _____ START TIME _____ END TIME _____
HIKE/TRAIL NAME _____ DURATION _____
LOCATION _____
TERRAIN _____
COMPANIONS _____

TRAIL CONDITIONS   WEATHER

TRAIL NOTES

5 THINGS I DISCOVERED ON THE TRAIL | TOP 5 THINGS I LIKE ABOUT THE TRAIL

SKETCH | PHOTO

DIFFICULTY     OVERALL RATING

DATE _____ START TIME _____ END TIME _____
HIKE/TRAIL NAME _____ DURATION _____
LOCATION _____
TERRAIN _____
COMPANIONS _____

TRAIL CONDITIONS
_____
_____
_____

WEATHER

TRAIL NOTES
_____
_____
_____
_____
_____

5 THINGS I DISCOVERED ON THE TRAIL	TOP 5 THINGS I LIKE ABOUT THE TRAIL

SKETCH	PHOTO

DIFFICULTY ☆ ☆ ☆ ☆ ☆ OVERALL RATING ☆ ☆ ☆ ☆ ☆

DATE _____   START TIME _____ END TIME _____
HIKE/TRAIL NAME _____   DURATION _____
LOCATION _____
TERRAIN _____
COMPANIONS _____

TRAIL CONDITIONS
_____
_____
_____

WEATHER

TRAIL NOTES
_____
_____
_____
_____
_____

5 THINGS I DISCOVERED ON THE TRAIL
_____
_____
_____
_____
_____

TOP 5 THINGS I LIKE ABOUT THE TRAIL
_____
_____
_____
_____
_____

SKETCH

PHOTO

DIFFICULTY ☆ ☆ ☆ ☆ ☆   OVERALL RATING ☆ ☆ ☆ ☆ ☆

DATE _____	START TIME _____ END TIME _____
HIKE/TRAIL NAME _____	DURATION _____

LOCATION _____
TERRAIN _____
COMPANIONS _____

TRAIL CONDITIONS
_____
_____
_____

WEATHER

TRAIL NOTES
_____
_____
_____
_____
_____

5 THINGS I DISCOVERED ON THE TRAIL	TOP 5 THINGS I LIKE ABOUT THE TRAIL
_____	_____
_____	_____
_____	_____
_____	_____
_____	_____

SKETCH	PHOTO

DIFFICULTY ☆ ☆ ☆ ☆ ☆ OVERALL RATING ☆ ☆ ☆ ☆ ☆

DATE _____ START TIME _____ END TIME _____
HIKE/TRAIL NAME _____ DURATION _____
LOCATION _____
TERRAIN _____
COMPANIONS _____

TRAIL CONDITIONS
_____
_____
_____

WEATHER

TRAIL NOTES
_____
_____
_____
_____
_____

5 THINGS I DISCOVERED ON THE TRAIL	TOP 5 THINGS I LIKE ABOUT THE TRAIL

SKETCH	PHOTO

DIFFICULTY  OVERALL RATING

DATE _____ START TIME _____ END TIME _____
HIKE/TRAIL NAME _____ DURATION _____
LOCATION _____
TERRAIN _____
COMPANIONS _____

TRAIL CONDITIONS

WEATHER

TRAIL NOTES

5 THINGS I DISCOVERED ON THE TRAIL

TOP 5 THINGS I LIKE ABOUT THE TRAIL

SKETCH

PHOTO

DIFFICULTY ☆ ☆ ☆ ☆ ☆ OVERALL RATING ☆ ☆ ☆ ☆ ☆

DATE _____ START TIME _____ END TIME _____
HIKE/TRAIL NAME _____ DURATION _____
LOCATION _____
TERRAIN _____
COMPANIONS _____

TRAIL CONDITIONS

_____
_____
_____

WEATHER

TRAIL NOTES

_____
_____
_____
_____
_____

5 THINGS I DISCOVERED ON THE TRAIL	TOP 5 THINGS I LIKE ABOUT THE TRAIL

SKETCH	PHOTO

DIFFICULTY   OVERALL RATING

DATE _____   START TIME _____ END TIME _____
HIKE/TRAIL NAME _____ DURATION _____
LOCATION _____
TERRAIN _____
COMPANIONS _____

TRAIL CONDITIONS   WEATHER
_____
_____
_____

TRAIL NOTES
_____
_____
_____
_____
_____

5 THINGS I DISCOVERED ON THE TRAIL	TOP 5 THINGS I LIKE ABOUT THE TRAIL

SKETCH	PHOTO

DIFFICULTY   OVERALL RATING

DATE _____ START TIME _____ END TIME _____
HIKE/TRAIL NAME _____ DURATION _____
LOCATION _____
TERRAIN _____
COMPANIONS _____

TRAIL CONDITIONS
_____
_____
_____

WEATHER

TRAIL NOTES
_____
_____
_____
_____
_____

5 THINGS I DISCOVERED ON THE TRAIL
_____
_____
_____
_____
_____

TOP 5 THINGS I LIKE ABOUT THE TRAIL
_____
_____
_____
_____
_____

SKETCH

PHOTO

DIFFICULTY ☆ ☆ ☆ ☆ ☆ OVERALL RATING ☆ ☆ ☆ ☆ ☆

DATE _____ START TIME _____ END TIME _____
HIKE/TRAIL NAME _____ DURATION _____
LOCATION _____
TERRAIN _____
COMPANIONS _____

TRAIL CONDITIONS
_____
_____
_____

WEATHER

TRAIL NOTES
_____
_____
_____
_____
_____

5 THINGS I DISCOVERED ON THE TRAIL	TOP 5 THINGS I LIKE ABOUT THE TRAIL

SKETCH	PHOTO

DIFFICULTY ☆ ☆ ☆ ☆ ☆ OVERALL RATING ☆ ☆ ☆ ☆ ☆

DATE _____ START TIME _____ END TIME _____
HIKE/TRAIL NAME _____ DURATION _____
LOCATION _____
TERRAIN _____
COMPANIONS _____

TRAIL CONDITIONS

WEATHER

TRAIL NOTES

5 THINGS I DISCOVERED ON THE TRAIL

TOP 5 THINGS I LIKE ABOUT THE TRAIL

SKETCH

PHOTO

DIFFICULTY ☆ ☆ ☆ ☆ ☆ OVERALL RATING ☆ ☆ ☆ ☆ ☆

DATE _____ START TIME _____ END TIME _____
HIKE/TRAIL NAME _____ DURATION _____
LOCATION _____
TERRAIN _____
COMPANIONS _____

TRAIL CONDITIONS
_____
_____
_____

WEATHER

TRAIL NOTES
_____
_____
_____
_____
_____

5 THINGS I DISCOVERED ON THE TRAIL	TOP 5 THINGS I LIKE ABOUT THE TRAIL
_____	_____
_____	_____
_____	_____
_____	_____
_____	_____

SKETCH	PHOTO

DIFFICULTY ☆ ☆ ☆ ☆ ☆ OVERALL RATING ☆ ☆ ☆ ☆ ☆

DATE _____ START TIME _____ END TIME _____
HIKE/TRAIL NAME _____ DURATION _____
LOCATION _____
TERRAIN _____
COMPANIONS _____

TRAIL CONDITIONS

_____
_____
_____

WEATHER

TRAIL NOTES

_____
_____
_____
_____
_____

5 THINGS I DISCOVERED ON THE TRAIL

_____
_____
_____
_____
_____

TOP 5 THINGS I LIKE ABOUT THE TRAIL

_____
_____
_____
_____
_____

SKETCH

PHOTO

DIFFICULTY    OVERALL RATING

DATE _____ START TIME _____ END TIME _____
HIKE/TRAIL NAME _____ DURATION _____
LOCATION _____
TERRAIN _____
COMPANIONS _____

TRAIL CONDITIONS
_____
_____
_____

WEATHER

TRAIL NOTES
_____
_____
_____
_____

5 THINGS I DISCOVERED ON THE TRAIL	TOP 5 THINGS I LIKE ABOUT THE TRAIL

SKETCH	PHOTO

DIFFICULTY ☆ ☆ ☆ ☆ ☆ OVERALL RATING ☆ ☆ ☆ ☆ ☆

DATE _____   START TIME _____ END TIME _____
HIKE/TRAIL NAME _____   DURATION _____
LOCATION _____
TERRAIN _____
COMPANIONS _____

TRAIL CONDITIONS
_____
_____
_____

WEATHER

TRAIL NOTES
_____
_____
_____
_____
_____

5 THINGS I DISCOVERED ON THE TRAIL	TOP 5 THINGS I LIKE ABOUT THE TRAIL

SKETCH

PHOTO

DIFFICULTY ☆ ☆ ☆ ☆ ☆ OVERALL RATING ☆ ☆ ☆ ☆ ☆

DATE _____ START TIME _____ END TIME _____
HIKE/TRAIL NAME _____ DURATION _____
LOCATION _____
TERRAIN _____
COMPANIONS _____

TRAIL CONDITIONS
_____
_____
_____

WEATHER

TRAIL NOTES
_____
_____
_____
_____
_____

5 THINGS I DISCOVERED ON THE TRAIL
_____
_____
_____
_____
_____

TOP 5 THINGS I LIKE ABOUT THE TRAIL
_____
_____
_____
_____
_____

SKETCH

PHOTO

DIFFICULTY    OVERALL RATING

DATE _____
HIKE/TRAIL NAME _____
LOCATION _____
TERRAIN _____
COMPANIONS _____

START TIME _____ END TIME _____
DURATION _____

TRAIL CONDITIONS

WEATHER

TRAIL NOTES

5 THINGS I DISCOVERED ON THE TRAIL

TOP 5 THINGS I LIKE ABOUT THE TRAIL

SKETCH

PHOTO

DIFFICULTY ☆ ☆ ☆ ☆ ☆ OVERALL RATING ☆ ☆ ☆ ☆ ☆

DATE _____	START TIME _____ END TIME _____
HIKE/TRAIL NAME _____	DURATION _____
LOCATION _____	
TERRAIN _____	
COMPANIONS _____	

TRAIL CONDITIONS

_____
_____
_____

WEATHER

TRAIL NOTES

_____
_____
_____
_____

5 THINGS I DISCOVERED ON THE TRAIL	TOP 5 THINGS I LIKE ABOUT THE TRAIL
_____	_____
_____	_____
_____	_____
_____	_____
_____	_____

SKETCH	PHOTO

DIFFICULTY ☆ ☆ ☆ ☆ ☆ OVERALL RATING ☆ ☆ ☆ ☆ ☆

DATE _____   START TIME _____ END TIME _____
HIKE/TRAIL NAME _____   DURATION _____
LOCATION _____
TERRAIN _____
COMPANIONS _____

TRAIL CONDITIONS
_____
_____

WEATHER

TRAIL NOTES
_____
_____
_____
_____

5 THINGS I DISCOVERED ON THE TRAIL	TOP 5 THINGS I LIKE ABOUT THE TRAIL

SKETCH	PHOTO

DIFFICULTY  OVERALL RATING

DATE _____ START TIME _____ END TIME _____
HIKE/TRAIL NAME _____ DURATION _____
LOCATION _____
TERRAIN _____
COMPANIONS _____

TRAIL CONDITIONS
_____
_____
_____

WEATHER

TRAIL NOTES
_____
_____
_____
_____

5 THINGS I DISCOVERED ON THE TRAIL	TOP 5 THINGS I LIKE ABOUT THE TRAIL

SKETCH	PHOTO

DIFFICULTY ☆ ☆ ☆ ☆ ☆ OVERALL RATING ☆ ☆ ☆ ☆ ☆

DATE _____ START TIME _____ END TIME _____
HIKE/TRAIL NAME _____ DURATION _____
LOCATION _____
TERRAIN _____
COMPANIONS _____

TRAIL CONDITIONS
_____
_____
_____

WEATHER

TRAIL NOTES
_____
_____
_____
_____
_____

5 THINGS I DISCOVERED ON THE TRAIL	TOP 5 THINGS I LIKE ABOUT THE TRAIL

SKETCH	PHOTO

DIFFICULTY ☆ ☆ ☆ ☆ ☆ OVERALL RATING ☆ ☆ ☆ ☆ ☆

DATE _____ START TIME _____ END TIME _____
HIKE/TRAIL NAME _____ DURATION _____
LOCATION _____
TERRAIN _____
COMPANIONS _____

TRAIL CONDITIONS
_____
_____
_____

WEATHER

TRAIL NOTES
_____
_____
_____
_____
_____

5 THINGS I DISCOVERED ON THE TRAIL	TOP 5 THINGS I LIKE ABOUT THE TRAIL

SKETCH	PHOTO

DIFFICULTY    OVERALL RATING

DATE _____ START TIME _____ END TIME _____
HIKE/TRAIL NAME _____ DURATION _____
LOCATION _____
TERRAIN _____
COMPANIONS _____

TRAIL CONDITIONS
_____
_____
_____

WEATHER

TRAIL NOTES
_____
_____
_____
_____

5 THINGS I DISCOVERED ON THE TRAIL	TOP 5 THINGS I LIKE ABOUT THE TRAIL

SKETCH	PHOTO

DIFFICULTY ☆ ☆ ☆ ☆ ☆ OVERALL RATING ☆ ☆ ☆ ☆ ☆

DATE _____ START TIME _____ END TIME _____
HIKE/TRAIL NAME _____ DURATION _____
LOCATION _____
TERRAIN _____
COMPANIONS _____

TRAIL CONDITIONS
_____
_____
_____

WEATHER

TRAIL NOTES
_____
_____
_____
_____
_____

5 THINGS I DISCOVERED ON THE TRAIL	TOP 5 THINGS I LIKE ABOUT THE TRAIL

SKETCH	PHOTO

DIFFICULTY ☆ ☆ ☆ ☆ ☆ OVERALL RATING ☆ ☆ ☆ ☆ ☆

DATE _____ START TIME _____ END TIME _____
HIKE/TRAIL NAME _____ DURATION _____
LOCATION _____
TERRAIN _____
COMPANIONS _____

TRAIL CONDITIONS

WEATHER

TRAIL NOTES

5 THINGS I DISCOVERED ON THE TRAIL

TOP 5 THINGS I LIKE ABOUT THE TRAIL

SKETCH

PHOTO

DIFFICULTY ☆ ☆ ☆ ☆ ☆ OVERALL RATING ☆ ☆ ☆ ☆ ☆

DATE _____ START TIME _____ END TIME _____
HIKE/TRAIL NAME _____ DURATION _____
LOCATION _____
TERRAIN _____
COMPANIONS _____

TRAIL CONDITIONS
_____
_____
_____

WEATHER

TRAIL NOTES
_____
_____
_____
_____

5 THINGS I DISCOVERED ON THE TRAIL	TOP 5 THINGS I LIKE ABOUT THE TRAIL
_____	_____
_____	_____
_____	_____
_____	_____
_____	_____

SKETCH	PHOTO

DIFFICULTY ☆ ☆ ☆ ☆ ☆ OVERALL RATING ☆ ☆ ☆ ☆ ☆

DATE _____ START TIME _____ END TIME _____
HIKE/TRAIL NAME _____ DURATION _____
LOCATION _____
TERRAIN _____
COMPANIONS _____

TRAIL CONDITIONS
_____
_____
_____

WEATHER

TRAIL NOTES
_____
_____
_____
_____

5 THINGS I DISCOVERED ON THE TRAIL	TOP 5 THINGS I LIKE ABOUT THE TRAIL

SKETCH

PHOTO

DIFFICULTY    OVERALL RATING

DATE _____ START TIME _____ END TIME _____
HIKE/TRAIL NAME _____ DURATION _____
LOCATION _____
TERRAIN _____
COMPANIONS _____

TRAIL CONDITIONS
_____
_____
_____

WEATHER

TRAIL NOTES
_____
_____
_____
_____
_____

5 THINGS I DISCOVERED ON THE TRAIL	TOP 5 THINGS I LIKE ABOUT THE TRAIL

SKETCH	PHOTO

DIFFICULTY ☆ ☆ ☆ ☆ ☆ OVERALL RATING ☆ ☆ ☆ ☆ ☆

DATE _____   START TIME _____ END TIME _____
HIKE/TRAIL NAME _____   DURATION _____
LOCATION _____
TERRAIN _____
COMPANIONS _____

TRAIL CONDITIONS
_____
_____

WEATHER

TRAIL NOTES
_____
_____
_____
_____

5 THINGS I DISCOVERED ON THE TRAIL	TOP 5 THINGS I LIKE ABOUT THE TRAIL

SKETCH	PHOTO

DIFFICULTY ☆ ☆ ☆ ☆ ☆ OVERALL RATING ☆ ☆ ☆ ☆ ☆

| DATE _____ | START TIME _____ END TIME _____ |
| HIKE/TRAIL NAME _____ | DURATION _____ |

LOCATION _____
TERRAIN _____
COMPANIONS _____

TRAIL CONDITIONS
_____
_____
_____

WEATHER

TRAIL NOTES
_____
_____
_____
_____

5 THINGS I DISCOVERED ON THE TRAIL	TOP 5 THINGS I LIKE ABOUT THE TRAIL
_____	_____
_____	_____
_____	_____
_____	_____
_____	_____

SKETCH	PHOTO

DIFFICULTY ☆ ☆ ☆ ☆ ☆ OVERALL RATING ☆ ☆ ☆ ☆ ☆

www.ingramcontent.com/pod-product-compliance
Lightning Source LLC
Chambersburg PA
CBHW071722020426
42333CB00017B/2364